From Lake Erie to the Pacific

From Lake Erie to the Pacific

LT j.g. Edward N. Cooper

Copyright © 2009 by Edward N. Cooper.

ISBN: Hardcover   978-1-4415-3484-2
       Softcover   978-1-4415-3483-5

All rights reserved. No part of this book may be reproduced or transmitted in any form or by any means, electronic or mechanical, including photocopying, recording, or by any information storage and retrieval system, without permission in writing from the copyright owner.

This book was printed in the United States of America.

To order additional copies of this book, contact:
Xlibris Corporation
1-888-795-4274
www.Xlibris.com
Orders@Xlibris.com
62118

Dedication:

I dedicate this book to my wonderful wife, Vivian, who did all the hard work and spent many, many hours putting it all together. After writing and getting eleven Western Novels Published, this is a new venture for her.

This is the story as told to me (Vivian Cooper) by my husband, then LT. j.g. Edward N. Cooper, U.S.N.R. He had always dreamed of being a pilot, from a small child, who watched his Hero (Milt Hershberger) fly a little red Waco picking up passengers and also doing loops, spinning and going around every which way, just acting crazy all over the sky.

    He graduated from high school and enlisted in the U.S.N.R. after the terrible tragedy of Pearl Harbor. He was elated when he qualified for flight training & eighteen months later he proudly received his gold Navy Wings. He went on to join the Squadron V.P.B. 13 and to fly the PB2Y-5, Coronado a large four engine flying boat, in the Pacific.

Have you ever heard of someone who seemed to have their head above the clouds? That was me. I was born and raised on a little Island out in Lake Erie, in Ohio, called "Put-in-Bay." This was a grape growing and wine making Island, and still is. It was always a vacation destination and that has greatly increased in recent years. My parents made wine and later had a restaurant there, but my story started when I was quite young.

I was a mischievous little kid, getting into much trouble. My mom had to tie me to the pear tree in the front yard to keep me from running out into the street. One time I got into the lard crock and greased my kiddy car. Oh yes, when I was very little I took a bolt out of my crib, put it in my mouth, and swallowed it. A couple days later I started to cry and my Mom called the doctor. He came to the house, and laid me on the kitchen table, and extracted it. When I started in the first grade I gave my teacher fits. One time she locked me in her coat closet. I found some Christmas cookies that someone had given her and I ate all of them. Boy—I was really in trouble!

Then, on an afternoon in mid-Feb. they left out school and we all marched down to the shore line of the Island park. We were told to watch in the sky to the East. Soon a little red speck appeared in the distance. It was a small open cockpit airplane and it landed on the ice right in front of us. How exciting, we had hardly ever seen an airplane. The pilot, dressed in heavy jacket, helmet, and goggles, jumped out and walked over to a group of men who had walked out on the ice. When that plane took off, I stood on tip toes and felt like butterflies were stampeding through my stomach. I took some deep breaths as I watched it disappear in the horizon. I never missed a day looking for that little red airplane.

The UPF—WACO

Somehow my Grandfather found out that I wanted a ride in that plane, I probably told him. Anyway, one day he asked me if I wanted to take a ride. I was so excited I almost jumped out of my britches, I couldn't wait! I felt I was ready to tackle the world and any planets that wanted to buy in the fight! We went out to that hay field and there was that little red airplane.

I didn't know what kind it was and I didn't care—I just wanted to go. (Later I was told it was a three-place straight wing waco.)

Standing alongside that Waco was a man in a leather jacket, with helmet and goggles. This man was Milton Hershberger who started what would later become "Island Airlines". I was lifted up into that front cockpit and sat on somebody's lap. My Grandfather did not go along, don't know if he ever flew. I sure was glad he paid that dollar for my ride. We took off and it was so noisy. Wow—I could see everywhere, I didn't know the world was so big. I could see all the Islands and boats on the lake, it was so exciting. From that day on—"I wanted to fly"!

As I got a little older and got a bicycle, I would ride out to the airport and watch the planes come and go. To see the pilot crawl into that rear cockpit, with passengers or freight in front—take off and disappear toward the Mainland—it just took my breath away.

Of course they had built a hanger but most of the floor was dirt. As business grew, improvements were made and a big old furnace was in one corner. In winter it was bitter cold working on those planes. Sometimes I'd go in the hanger and watch the mechanic. He was a nice guy but I knew I had to stay out of the way. Milt had acquired a three-place Travelair and one or two five place New Standards. The Standards were open cockpit with four passengers up front facing each other. By then he had hired another pilot. The only accident that I can recall in those early days was when his pilot, Bill Smogy, left the Mainland on a early spring morning in one of the Standards with two passengers aboard. He ran into a fog bank as he was nearing the Put-in-Bay Airport and went into the icy lake. People at the Airport could hear the cries for help but no one could get to them in time.

Going back a bit—The reason this Airline was so vital to the Island was that in the winter time, crossing the lake to the Mainland was very treacherous. They used large wooden row boats, covered with sheet metal, and on runners. They were called "Ironclads" and were pulled by two men. If the ice was good it was ok, but when there were open spots in the lake, they put the boats in the water and rowed. This was usually wet and cold. That is how passengers and Freight and mail were transported. Needless to say, not many of the Island folks traveled in winter unless the ice was good enough to drive a car across. The Catholic Priest who served the **Islands** was very much involved with Milt. in providing Air Service. He would have Mass on one Island one Sunday and another Island the next Sunday. By flying he could have Mass on two Islands every Sunday. Rev. Joseph Maerder was nick named, "The flying Bishop"!

Milt was also able to secure the Mail contract serving the Islands. To Honor the first Air Mail flight, many important people came to the Island. Somehow my dad became involved in this and they all met at our home. (Maybe they wanted to sample some good Island wine). Among the group was a man named Walter Hinton. He was a Naval Aviator and one of the first to fly the Atlantic in a Curtiss N.C. flying boat in 1919. People had gathered to celebrate the opening of Island Airlines. Several planes flew in, along with a lady in an Auto Gyro. I, being the only little kid around, got to shake their hands. (How ironic that year's later I too would be a Naval Aviator piloting flying boats. I would always watch for planes and dream that someday I might be up there flying one. When I was in High School I had all the literature on "Piper Cubs". They sold for $1270.00. I wanted one the worst way. I knew my Parents didn't have that kind of money, but I still dreamed. Perhaps my grades would have been better if my mind had been on my school work. Before I graduated from High School came that awful day, "Pearl Harbor" Now it dawned on me that maybe I would fly one of Uncle Sam's planes, if I was accepted into the Navy, which I had decided to do . . .

In September of 1942 I went to Columbus, Ohio to enlist in Naval Aviation. I felt the drum roll of raised emotions, realizing

I was going all by myself to do something that would no doubt change my life forever. I went to the mainland and with those butterflies in my stomach, I boarded the bus for Columbus. You had better believe I was nervous as I got to the Recruiting headquarters along with several other guys. Most of the first day was paper work—I never answered so many questions in school. Then a fellow interviewed me, he was wearing a pair of "Gold Wings" which really took my eyes. I wondered if I would ever be able to wear one of those, but I thought, only the "Good Lord" knew. The next day they gave me a physical exam. They checked things I didn't even know I had. Then the Color Blind tests—I thought you just had to be able to see and I didn't have any problem with that as far as I knew. They put you in a special chair and spun you around like a top to test your vertigo—That was one time I was glad I was used to riding the rough waters of Lake Erie and I didn't even get sick. I was finally sent down the hall to an office to get the results of these tests. I reasoned my first solo flight couldn't make me this nervous. I stood at the door for a few seconds until I could get courage enough to open it. I was shocked when I heard the words, "You passed"! Then he said—"except for one little thing." "Oh, no", what now? My legs felt weak and I held on to the counter as he finished, "Your left eye is not quite 20/20 and a perfect eye sight is required. I suggest you go home for a week, wear sun glasses, eat carrots, and take Vitamin A pills." He laughed as he added, "Also don't look at too many girls."

 I was a pretty excited, relieved, kid as I caught the next bus for home. Believe me, I did everything they said and the local grocer must have thought I was raising rabbits as I always had a carrot in my hand. The sun glasses must have made me look like a movie star. The worst part about it was not being able to look at the girls. (It might be a strange coincidence but my cousin who was a B-24 Pilot in the Air Force had to go through the same ordeal) A week later I again took a bus ride to Columbus—and I passed! I was sworn into "The United States Naval Reserve." The first part of my dream had come true! I was ecstatic. I returned to the Island and I needed a job until I was called up. I was fortunate and overjoyed as I went to work for that Barnstormer who had given me my first airplane ride. He was my boyhood "Hero" and now he was encouraging me in every way he could. He was now operating three Ford Tri-motors and his company was called "Island Airlines," which served the Islands of Lake Erie. It was a nine minute flight from Put-in-Bay to Port Clinton—the Mainland Terminal. They had the year around mail contract and in the winter when there was no boat service—the airline carried most everything. Drums of gas, sacks of coal, Bales of hay, or a Casket—all in a day's work. I sold tickets, hustled freight, hauled mail to the Post Offices, and got to do a lot of airplane riding. I was called up in Jan. of 43' and reported to Detroit, Mich. I had been told that I probably would go to Bowling Green, Ohio for my first three months of training. This is great, I thought, as its only 40 or 50 miles from home. I'd get to go home on weekends, too. So, I took very little with me and told my folks I'd see them in a week. Boy, was I wrong, as that week lasted 15 months.

They checked us in and then told us—"Sorry guys, but you are going to Seattle, Washington." This had not been done before, but there was a change and we were to take three months of ground school before our flight training. This was my first train ride—ever—and it wasn't bad. We were in regular Pullman cars with good food and a bed. Of course we took the northern route and even though it was winter, it was still scenic. When the train would stop, we would get off for a couple minutes & then back on. I remember in Montana, or somewhere, we hopped off and the conductor hollered at us to get back on before we froze. We were in our shirt sleeves and with that dry, clear air you didn't realize it was 25 degrees below zero.

It took us about four days to arrive in Seattle and were bused to the University of Washington. They put us in the girl's dorm, which was empty. Now we got our first taste of Navy life, we were issued uniforms and had to salute. We had ground school classes 5 days a week & sometimes 6—all day & sometimes in the evenings. There was no time for anything except study, study. That was o.k.—we knew it wouldn't be a picnic. We went out to drill before 6 a.m. chow and sometimes that wasn't too nice. Seattle is "wet" in the winter and when it's not raining, its foggy, or both. I swear sometimes you could just see a slit in the fog where the cadets ahead of you had marched. We studied lots of math, communications (code semaphore, & blinker), navigation, etc. Oh yes there was physical training too, to get us in shape. I can only remember leaving the campus twice in those three months. One time We went to Seattle to see a movie with Lena Horne starring in it. I thought she was the most beautiful woman there was. Maybe because we didn't see many girls as we were not allowed to fraternize with the college students. (We didn't have time anyway.) Yes, we learned how to stand watch—even though we were living in a dorm. It was an interesting three months and I'm sure it was beneficial training. A few didn't make it though. Next they moved us to Gonzaga University in Spokane, Wash.

Now we were really excited, we would get to fly. Once again we were housed in a girl's dorm. (No girls or urinals). It was about the same setup as at the U of W. The weather here was much nicer, of course it was spring and nearing summer. Here half the day was ground school and P.T. and the other half flying.

We were bussed to an airport called "Felts Field," not much commercial traffic at the time—mostly flight schools. Here I was introduced to the first airplane I would fly, a 65 H.P. Taylor craft. This was much like the Piper Cubs I had dreamed about in High School. (As I go through this story from here on, various names, times, and places will be taken from my Flight Log Books—My memory is not that good). My first instructor was Bob Vandervert—a tall slim fellow with cowboy boots. He may well have come off the ranch, but he was a good instructor. The first couple duals went pretty well, so he traded me over to a young lady instructor. I do not remember her name but I sure remember what she looked like, she was "very friendly,"—enough said! One day we were flying and my parachute harness came off my left shoulder. She said—"Honey, did your brassiere strap fall down?" I was too busy flying to follow up on that. Anyway, after 7 hours of dual, she told me to stop at the end of the run-way and let her off. "Oh my gosh, I've got to do this by myself! She told me just to take it around once and come back and pick her up. I don't know which part of me was trembling the most, but do you know, when I advanced that throttle, all fear was gone. I felt like the Lord in Heaven had HIS hand on my shoulder. I circled the field once and probably made as good a landing as I've ever made. I stopped and picked up my lady instructor and she was all smiles. She said, "Well, Ed, you did it! Take me back to the flight line and let me out. You shoot a few landings, I'll see you back in a half hour!" It was a thrilling day, I'll never forget it. Training continued with both dual and solo flights. We practiced basic maneuvers, simulated forced landings, and lots of touch and go landings. After about forty hours Mr. Vandervert gave me my final check ride and the first phase of my training was complete . . .

Our training then moved across the field to where they had almost the exact airplane that I had my first ride in when I was six years old. Here we flew 220 H.P. open cockpit Waco Biplanes. Oh! I could hardly wait, this would be fun.

My instructor was Andy Gibney, a great guy. He introduced me to the Waco and said—"Let's go." Quite different then the T. Craft but I took to it pretty well. Two hours of dual, then came the instructors words that you were waiting for—"Let me out!" I got over 20 hours Waco time. We did some spins and loops but really didn't get into aerobatics. When I later got to Livermore I appreciated this Waco time as it got me ready for the Stearman that was lighter and easier to fly. Oh yes, one side note I must add, when I was at U of W. my roommate was a big fellow from Mchigan. "Curtiss Copeland." He was still my roommate at Gonzaga. We did get into town once in a while on weekends and somewhere along the way we met a couple gals that liked to ride horses. We went riding with them a couple of times. I never really mastered the art of going up and down when the horse did. (Give me an airplane).

Our fun of flying was now over for three months and we headed for St. Mary's College in California. We took the train from Spokane to Oakland and then they bussed us to St. Mary's. We knew this was going to be tough. Several friends washed out, we always hated to see that. (The term washed out means that a cadet was terminated from the flight program. Some stayed in the Navy and others transferred to the Air Force or their branches of service. Copeland and I were again room mates—that's odd unless it was because both our names started with "Co." Pre-flight consisted of ground school and much very vigorous physical training. Running the "obstacle course" was a killer, everyone hated it. We did not play tennis or golf, it was physical training, Wrestling, boxing, running, swimming, climbing walls and cargo nets, tumbling, etc. This went on every day. I actually enjoyed the cross country running and I did quite well at it. About this time I acquired something like a boil on my right side belt line. It became infected and I was sent to the Naval Hospital in Oakland. They swabbed it out and killed the infection. I guess I was there four or five days then I went back to St. Mary's.

Even though I was born on an Island in Lake Erie, I didn't know how to swim. I had to work every day in the summer and never got to go swimming with the other kids. I can remember twice I went down to the docks with the other kids. Since I couldn't swim, they threw me in and I panicked, so they had to come and get me. Needless to say, I had a fear of the water.

At pre-flight school I was told, "If you don't swim you don't fly." I knew I had to swim or wash out. When I came up to the swimming part of the training I worked very hard—I had a great fear when my head was under water. Apparently I was blessed to have instructors who were helpful and patient with me.

Remember, we had tough Navy and Marine instructors and they *were tough.* I soon learned the crawl, backstroke, breaststroke and 100' under water with my clothes on. We had to learn the life saving carries and I did that too. Boxing came up—which I hated—and they let me stay in swimming to pass all my tests. I tell you, once more the LORD had HIS Hand on me. I passed every test and I actually enjoyed swimming under the water more then on top. Ground school was tough too—I was thankful for my good High school education, even though it took me thirteen years to do it.

Discipline was very strict at pre-flight—they made sure you learned to do things the "Navy Way." Square corners on the beds, shoes shined, uniforms spotless, and always ready for "White Glove" inspections. Yes it was tough—but for those who made it through—it was a very happy day. I believe I went to Oakland twice on weekend leave—it was mostly keeping our noses to the grindstone. How could anyone want to fly so bad—"But I did."

Now we were ready once more to head for the clouds. We transferred over to Livermore Naval Air Station, which really wasn't that far away. What a beautiful sight when we arrived and saw all those "Beautiful," yellow Stearman Bi-planes lined up on the flight line, talk about "chompin' at the bit" to get flying. Of course it took a few days, as we had to go through indoctrination and get started with more ground school. (Ground school and P.T. were always part of the program everywhere you went.)

November 6, 1943 was my first dual flight in a Stearman. My instructor was a Marine Captain and he was tough. He was very good but he didn't want to see the same mistake twice. Livermore wasn't like an airport, it did not have runways. It had a large square asphalt mat—probably 12 or 15 planes could land side by side at one time. "Airplanes were as thick as flies on a horse biscuit." Believe it or not, there wasn't any radio communication—the control tower kept things in order by flashing a light at you. A green light meant go or cleared to land—yellow was proceed with caution. Red meant stop if you were on the ground or, don't land if you were in the air. Why there weren't anymore accidents I'll never know. I don't recall any at the field. Most flights lasted from 1 hour to 1 ½ hrs. Back in Spokane we had civilian instructors, but now they were all Navy and Marine pilots. (I must add, no women) I guess they were more cautious as I had 10 hrs. dual before my solo check ride. So, on the 14th I got to go it alone again. It wasn't like the first solo, but it was a good feeling.

Training continued and every 3rd or 4th flight would be a dual.

After 20 hrs. I came up for my "B" stage check ride and I was "Blessed" with a new "Hot Shot" Ensign who failed me. Then I had to pass two more check rides, which I did. Up until now it was just learning to fly and shooting lots of landings. Now things were getting a bit more precise. Landings had to be on the spot and maneuvers had to come out where they were supposed to. I did o.k. and passed my "C" check. Now we were in aerobatics and formation flying. I loved flying upside down, just hanging on to the seat belt. I'd climb up to about 5,000 ft., roll over, and just glide back down to 1,500 ft . . . Of course the fuel was gravity fed from tanks in the upper wing and when you stayed upside down for any period of time the engine would quit. The prop would continue to windmill and, fortunately for me, it always restarted when I rolled back to the right position. I must say I put all caution to the wind when having so much fun.

About this time we had a very severe wind storm one night and we were all called out of our beds about 1 A.M. to report to the flight line. Even though the planes were tied down there were several cadets stationed at each plane to help hold them down. We were actually in a sand storm, it was even tough to breathe.

We had our flight goggles on and they along with the paint on the planes, were severely sand blasted.

Also about this time it was Christmas 1943—my first Christmas away from home. I went on weekend leave to Oakland with a couple of my buddies. It was fine, except on Christmas day they had invites out, and I didn't. I spent it in the hotel alone and that was not much fun! You would have thought they could have been more thoughtful.

"D" stage continued and I had one Dual flight with Lt. Robert Taylor (the movie star). We would sometimes take members of the ground crew along on our solo flights, so that they would be able to collect flight pay. It was fun to do a lot of aerobatics to see if you could make them sick. Hopefully their "heave" would not come flying back into your face!

Unfortunately, because of all this playing around & not practicing what I was suppose to—I failed my "D" stage check ride. Once again I had to ask for extra time—and then I was able to pass 2 "D" check rides. (I think they were beginning to lose patience with me).

Not far from Livermore there was a "Navy lighter than air" Base—this is where they trained "Blimp Pilots." (The Blimps were used to patrol along our Coastlines for submarines, etc.) Many of those learning to fly "Blimps" were Cadets who had washed out of our training program. I'm sure many of them could fly as well as we did, but something didn't go right with them. We loved to go over to their training area and "Buzz" around them. This was absolutely "forbidden," but we did it anyway. Some of our boys who got caught were washed out, unfortunately.

We went into stage "F" which was night flying. That went quite well, it consisted mostly of shooting landings—we didn't venture too far from the field. It was during this phase that I lost a good friend—he crashed and burned. As if that wasn't enough, they put the wreckage of his plane right next to the chow hall. I guess they thought it would remind us what "not to do." The smell of that wreckage sure didn't help your appetite any. It took me awhile to get over that loss and I was glad to be kept busy so my mind didn't dwell on it. On Jan. 22nd 1944 I took my final check and passed. That gave me 108 hrs. in the Stearman.

We then were transferred to Naval Air Station Corpus Christi, Texas where we were supposed to finish our training and get our wings. We were taken to "Cuddihy Field"—one of the outlying training fields. Of course wherever you went you always had ground school and P.T. Also at this time we were asked to make two decisions. Did we want to be a Navy or a Marine Pilot—and what kind of plane did we prefer. I asked for Navy and Multi-engine. I was fortunate and got both requests—that did not always happen.

We were introduced to the SNV—also known as the Vultee BT 13 "Vibrator." It was a low wing metal monoplane with a 450 HP engine. We thought it was great stuff, even though it was a long ways from being a fighter. After 4 hrs. of dual I passed my check ride and was once again flying solo. This was to become the last Navy plane that I would fly solo. We flew about 30 hrs just learning how to fly the plane. It was our last chance to goof off a bit & we used it to "chase tail" around the beautiful fluffy white clouds that were in the area. We thought this was fun

IT WAS March 1944 and I got my first leave to go home. I think they gave us two weeks, but none of us had the money to buy a plane or train ticket. (I didn't want to call my folks, I wanted to surprise them). We wanted to hitch a ride on a Military plane, but none were leaving our area. We were told we had to have our own parachutes to hitch a ride, so we checked out our parachutes at the Base. We pooled our money, hired a cab, and headed for Randolph Air Base. Of course we were all going different directions, but I found out that there was a C 46 transport leaving soon for Louisville, Ky. I jumped at the chance and hopped aboard. Of course I had my flight bag and a parachute. Guess what, this plane was equipped to carry troops and each bench seat had a chute. Anyway, we had very few passengers aboard. The ride to Louisville wasn't too comfortable, but we couldn't complain. On arrival, I called my uncle Herb, who lived across the river in Cincinnati. He was quite surprised to hear from me and told me what bus to take to get closer to him. He picked me up at the bus station and we had a very pleasant evening.

Early the next morning I caught another bus that would take me north to Port Clinton, Ohio. I arrived there about noon and took a cab the few miles to the airport. (I was about broke.) This was the mainland terminal for "Island Airlines" that flew to Put-in-Bay, my Island home town. I called Milt Hersberger, my old boss, and asked when the next flight was. His answer was, "Ed, you stay right there, I'll be over"! In addition to the Ford Tri-Motors, he was still flying an open cockpit "Standard." In just a few minutes that old Bi-plane appeared. He never shut it down, he just hollered, "Hop in,

Ed." We flew that long nine minute trip to the Island, what a joy. "I felt like the cat that had swallowed the canary" He shook my hand, wanted to know what I had been doing, and told me to get into his truck. He took me home, wished me well, and wouldn't take a penny—that's what my old barnstormer friend did for me.

My folks did not know I was coming home. I know now I should have told them. My dad was in the garden, working. When he saw me, he threw his tool in the air, he could have had a heart attack. We walked into the house and my mom almost fainted, she had to hang on to the kitchen sink. I'm sure neither one of them wanted me to fly, but they never apposed it as they knew that's what I wanted to do. In her letters, she would say "Ed, don't fly too high or too fast." Little did she know that if you fly—low and slow you get killed. I got two letters a week ever since I was gone, about 15 months, but they never really expressed their feelings. My brother left before I did and he was in Alaska. Maybe I shouldn't say this, but I was their baby who had hardly ever been away from home.

I had a great leave—that home cooking and my old bed felt so good. "I felt like a schoolboy on a holiday", but time flew and it was time to leave. My folks bought me a bus ticket to Corpus Christi and I was on my way.

Next we moved to Mainside at Corpus Christi where we started instrument training in the SNV. We also spent a lot of Link Trainer time "under the hood"! This was trying at times, but I enjoyed it and did o.k. After about 25 hrs. of Dual Instrument Time, I took my check ride with an "Ens. Cooper" and he passed me. I was so happy and I just ran from the Flight Line to the Hanger. The door was closed and I hit it with my right hand to open it. I hit it too high and my hand went through the window, which had wire mesh imbedded in it. It really sliced into my hand and wrist and they rushed me to the Emergency room. They had to sew nerves and blood vessels back together—I was a mess. What would happen, I was to start my twin engine training in a few days.

That accident happened on May 9th, 44 and as luck would have it we did not fly for almost two months. The weather turned bad and the clouds would blow in from the gulf and then they would blow back for a couple days. This went on for weeks, they had never seen such weather. It happened for so long a period Corpus Christi got an awful back log of Cadets needing to fly, so they finally decided to send some to Pensacola. (Of course this was giving my hand a chance to heal). The end of June we boarded a train—Cattle cars with flat wheels—and headed for Pensacola. (It was a ride to remember for many days to come). We arrived at the Main Station and were bussed to Whiting Field, near Milton, Fla., where we were to take our Twin Engine Training. Our quarters were 4 to a room, but it wasn't bad. The chow Hall was close by, which was nice. We were introduced to the SNB-2, Twin Beach. I thought it was a pretty aeroplane and I came to really enjoy flying it. As I mentioned before, my solo flying was over—you don't fly Twin Engine planes alone. After a few days of ground school and indoctrination, we had our first flight. The normal routine was, instructor and 2 or 3 students. The flights would last 2 1/2 to 3 hours, each taking his turn at flying, or riding back in the passenger area. Flying a Twin was a new experience and the first plane with a retractable landing gear. After we got the feel of the plane, we shot lots of landings. (No more aerobatics, the fun was over!) The normal schedule was to fly every other day, with every other weekend off. It was summer in Florida, hot and humid. When we had time off we usually went to Pensacola Beach and went swimming. One weekend I got very sunburned, I blistered before I left the beach. I couldn't take a shower and it was awful to wear a shirt. I had to keep up my flying and it was tough. In those days, it was a "court marshal" offence to not fly because of sunburn—if you had V.D. it was o.k.!

There were girls there, "Wow"—but I never remember having a date. (This would change after I got my wings.)

It was the 5th of July, 1944 when I had my first flight in the Twin Beach, on the 24th of August I took my check ride and passed, that was another happy day. I loved flying the Twin Beach, but it was not the easiest to handle on the ground. Of course it was a tail dragger and was very prone to ground looping. Also the landing gear was not very strong and with rough landings it would fail. It was not uncommon to see one come in with the wheels up, on the grass along side of the runway.

A couple days later, two of us Cadets got to take a ride by ourselves. That was nice, not having an instructor looking over your shoulder. This went on for a couple hops and then we had a couple more Duals. I believe this came about as they knew I was a bit "shook-up."

About three weeks before, one of my roommate's washed out on his navigation training. (Yes we still had ground school and P.T . . .) Then two weeks later, my other two roommates got killed in a mid-air collision. One evening, they didn't come back to the room after their flight. On my way to chow, I heard there had been an accident and six had gotten killed. I immediately went to the flight office to find out more. Yes, it was my two roommates, a kid from the next room, and their instructor. Also a student and instructor in a single engine trainer were killed. Needless to say, I did not go to the chow hall. I went back to the room, I was in pretty sad shape. I was alone in the room, all my buddies were gone! I asked myself, "What was going to happen to me? Would I wash out, would I get killed, or would I make it. My mind went back to my High School days and how I had saved pictures of the plane I wanted to own, I was so excited about flying and had been ever since I was small. This was my dream, always. I never thought about doing anything else with my life. How could things be so bad? I begin to pray and I asked the Lord, "Please help me make it!" Feeling some relief, I thought about the accident. It was evident the small plane was making a simulated instrument approach to the field, while my friends were also making their approach. Apparently they did not see each other.

A couple days later I was called in and asked if I would accompany the remains of my one roommate back to his home for the funeral. I was shown a container the size of a cigar box. They said that was it, there would be no casket. There was nothing left but a half melted and twisted dog tags—not much else. As I was preparing to leave they got a call from his mom. She had decided to have the Navy bury him in the Navy cemetery. I couldn't understand why but it did save me from a very unwanted trip.

We got back to flying—all that was left were a few "Cross Country flights. We flew to St Louis and back a couple of times and flew a few flights over the gulf. We had to find a Navy ship and return. The last flight, on the 12th of Sept., three of us Cadets were on our own. We flew a little over 3 hr. flight and were very happy to get back on the ground. We were finished, our training was over.

We spent a few days catching up on loose ends and getting our new uniforms. We also got cards showing that we had completed our training as Naval Aviators—and also our instrument rating. How proud we were and "How I thanked God that HE had answered my prayers and allowed me to make it through all of that training!"

The 26th of Sept. 1944 was a day to remember, we wore our Officers uniforms for the first time. Sparkling white, with a gold stripe on our shoulders and an Officer's cap—we looked sharp! But the most important of all was missing, "Our Wings!" We marched out onto the field and stood at attention, noone hardly breathed. The band started to play and the Navy "Brass" appeared. One after the other, we moved forward and were presented our Wings. That was it—a day never to be forgotten! We were told that less than 50% of those who started when we did, made it to Graduation.

The next day we got our "Orders". Mine read, "After a 30 day leave, transportation furnished, I would report to N.A.S. Shawnee, Okla. for more Navigation Training! Some of my gear was shipped direct, what I needed, I took with me. No parachute to drag along this time, I took a bus. It seemed to take forever but I finally made it to the airport in Port Clinton. It was late afternoon and I was just in time for the last trip of the Ford Tri—Motor, Just like old times when I worked for the airline before leaving for Service. This time my folks knew I was coming and met me at the airport.

It was great to be home again. My folks operated a small winery and grape picking and pressing were about over, I got in on a little of it. Quite a surprise, when I found out that my cousin, an Army Air Corp. B-24 pilot, was also home. It was great to compare notes. He had joined up before I did, he was older, and was about to leave for the European Theatre. It was great, but again the time just slipped away. Soon I was headed off to Shawnee, got there about the first of Nov.

Our quarters and Ground School was at "Oklahoma Baptist University." (This time we were in a boy's dorm.) The Navy had decided that all Multi Engine pilots must also be Navigators. Our flying was done from their City Airport, and we were again using the S.N.B. We didn't have much P.T. but did have a lot of very intensive Ground School. We flew a cross country flight every two or three days, an instructor and two students. Actually this training was much different from what I ended up doing. (There is very little ocean in the mid-west.) Denver was a very popular place to go. Oklahoma was a "dry" state, so we would stop and pick up a couple cases of booze. We had rented a meeting room and made it into an Officer's Club. In fact that's where I celebrated my 21st Birthday on the 26th of Nov. I also met a very nice lady whose husband had been killed in the Army in Europe. We almost got married after the war, but it wasn't to be.

This training lasted just a month, by now I had logged just 300 hrs . . . My orders came through to report to N.A.S. North Island, at San Diego, Calif. I was to join Squadron V.P.B. 100 as a pilot—Navigator on a PB2Y. This is a very large 4 Engine Flying Boat, not land based as I had hoped for.

Once again I was on a bus, headed for San Diego. In those days there was no bridge, so we were hauled across the Bay on a Navy Ferry. I reported in, was assigned quarters, and was told there would not be much doing for a few days. We would report in the morning, then be told to take the day off. After about ten days, they started to organize the Squadron. There were some who had already been out in the Pacific, but many were fresh out of training. I was assigned to a crew with pilots, Lt. George Saxon and Lt. Chuck Dill. George was a 90 day wonder, a spoiled brat from Tenn. Chuck was a great guy, we hit it off well. Chuck had been an enlisted man and had worked his way up through the ranks. He then took pilot training and was commissioned. We also had 9 enlisted men in the crew. Mansfield, our head Mechanic, was really a sharp guy. (You will learn later how he saved our necks). We also had 4 Ordnance men—one manned the Bomb Sight and the others manned the nose, top, & tail turrets, 2 radio men and 2 Ast. Mechanics made up the rest of the crew. Most were cross trained and were very capable of more than one job.

Even though there were lots of Navy personal stationed in the San Diego area, it was still a pretty good liberty town. When not on duty, we could come and go as we pleased. There never seemed to be any shortage of girls, including quite a few W.A.V.E.S. stationed at North Island. When one of our crews shipped out, their gals seemed ready to join another crew who were still in training!

We had many briefings and much Ground School. For those of us that had never seen a PB2Y before, there was much to learn. This was one of the largest planes flying at that time. It was strictly a Flying Boat—no wheels. At North Island there were ramps that sloped into the water. Men in wet suits would swim out with the Beaching Gear (wheels) and attach them to the hull, then a tractor would pull the plane up the ramp and to its parking spot.

On Jan. 19th, 45 we had our first training flight. Of course, being the Jr. pilot, I was not on the Flight Deck the first few flights. After that, we took turns—at least for take offs and landings. We flew 5 flights in Jan. with an Instructor pilot, getting acquainted with the plane. The Squadron had several different planes, you never knew which one you would fly. Most flights were 3 to 5 hrs. long. In Feb. we flew every other day, a lot of the time doing take-offs and landings. Our planes had Curtis-Electric Propellers, which means that the pitch of the prop was controlled by a small electric motor in the Hub of the Prop. These motors sometimes failed, the Prop would go into flat pitch, and you would have what was called, "a run a way Prop." When this happened, you immediately had to pull back all power and stop your take off run.

One time this happened when we were just ready to go airborne and the Wing Floats were already retracted. The head Mechanic sensed what was happening and opened the Top Hatch. He shouted for some of the crew to follow him up on top of the plane. They ran back and forth on top of the plane, balancing it, until the floats got back down. As luck would have it, we had a passenger aboard, who got very scared when he heard all the commotion. There was a hatch on the bottom of the plane, in the rear, that was used to throw out Smoke Bombs, Flares, etc. He opened that hatch, I guess he was going to jump out. Anyway, as we started to taxi back to the ramp, somebody yelled—"We're taking on water!" We stopped, closed the Hatch, and bailed water. Needless to say, that guy never flew with us again.

One day, while flying south along the coast, we thought we were seeing things. We were not a very fast plane—but we were passed by a small plane with its prop feathered (not turning). This is done on Multi engine planes if you lose an engine, the prop is set parallel to direction of flight to reduce drag. We later found out this plane had a jet engine. This was a test flight and they would use the prop engine if the jet failed.

Take offs and landings with a sea plane are much different then with a land plane. Take—offs are work, especially if the water is calm. After starting your take-off run, you actually have to rock the plane to break it loose from the water and get it up on the step to gain speed for take-off. If it's a little choppy there isn't near the problem.

This might be a good time to say that even though you have a flying boat, you can't just land it in the ocean wherever you please. When the swells get over 8 feet to 10 feet, it gets rough. We must land into the wind and that normally means, head on into the waves. If you bury your nose into a good one, you've had it!

We started practicing night landings and that is different. Even though you have landing lights, depth perception over the water is very difficult. You pretty much have to set up a rate of descent and wait to touch down on the water. Most of our night work was done at Salton Sea, an Inland body of water across the mountains and east of San Diego. This is a large salt water lake with almost no activity in the area. We used two flame pots to give us something to line up on for our landings. Not many people lived around the lake at that time, but there was a little farming done. One night, one of our planes that went over to shoot landings, saw a couple lights on a farm road. They mistook them for the flame pots on the lake and made their approach. It was to late when they realized there was no water. They made a beautiful landing, but as the plane quickly slowed, one wing float dug into the sand and the plane cart wheeled to the left. The wing was torn off and the plane was quite badly damaged. No one was injured but there were a few very red faces when the crew showed up back at North Island. The engines and some parts were salvaged—the rest was left. Maybe the farmer used it for a "chicken coop"!

We did some practice instrument flying and also several practice Bombing Flights. Bombs and Depth Charges were carried externally, under the wings, aft of the engines. This really affected the performance of the plane, it was like flying a large "barn door"!

On April 6th, 2 1/2 months after our training started, we received our own plane. S.N. 7163 was pretty much like we had been flying, only a few minor things to get used to. We did a couple test flights, a night Navigation hop, and then our simulated "Trans-Pac". "Trans-Pac" was the term used for the flight from San Diego to Hawaii.

This was a ten hour flight, 5 hrs. out and then turn around and come back to North Island. The flight was uneventful, no problems. Keep in mind, all this flying we had done with our New Plane was probably under 3,000 ft. altitude. We had not even gone over the mountains to Salton Sea.

On our second test flight, just after take off, we had a mid-air collision with a sea gull. Bird strikes can be dangerous if they hit the wind shield. If that bird had been a little bit higher I would no doubt have had glass and bird guts in my face. The only damage was a dent in the metal which was easily repaired.

They now installed Aux. Fuel tanks in the hull of our plane so we had extra fuel for that long flight. They also installed the "J.A.T.O" bottles. These are metal canisters about twice the size of a milk can. They contain a propellant, that when electrically fired off, give you a boast for take-off. They are used for heavy load or taking off in very rough seas. After you are airborn you release the bottles and they fall into the ocean.

On the evening of April 15th, 9 days after we received our plane, we took off and headed for Kaneohe, Hawaii. Everything went well, we flew about 1,000 ft. for about five hours, lightening our fuel load before we climbed to a higher altitude. We decided about 10,000 ft. would be our best cruising altitude for the remainder of the flight. We started a normal climb and just as we started to level off, "all four engines quit!" Believe me, if you haven't been there you don't know what it's like! As I mentioned before in this story, Chas. Mansfield was our head mechanic and he was the "best". He was sitting at his panel behind the pilot's seat, and immediately went into action. He knew it was loss of fuel and he immediately started pumping the hand "Wobble" pump. Airplanes of that size and that heavy just do not fly well with no propellers turning. I was back at the Navigation table, Saxon and Dill were flying. They pushed the nose down and put the plane into a rather steep glide, they kept it flying. Remember, its pitch black out and nothing around but 1,000 miles of water. The four props continued to windmill and with fuel pressure being restored with that hand pump, the engines coughed and restarted. The Altimeter was still unwinding like crazy, the ocean was coming at us fast. When they got us leveled off and flying again, we were less than 1,000 ft. Boy, was that close!

There is no way you could make a "dead stick" landing at sea, at night. We would have crashed and disappeared, we didn't have time to send out a "May-day" call. "Thank you, Lord, for saving us!"

Now we radioed San Diego and told them what happened. We told them we were coming back and had stayed about 1,000 ft. and just hoped those fans would keep running. Mansfield never took his hand off that pump the whole return trip and everyone was very alert. We did not buckle on our chutes as we were too low to use them, but everyone had on their life jackets—just in case. About an hour out of San Diego we called in and gave them our E.T.A. (Estimated Time of Arrival). They informed us that the harbor was fogged in and we would have to go over the mountains to Salton Sea. Our immediate answer was "no!" We could not chance climbing to that altitude and having our engines quit again. (By this time Mansfield had diagnosed the problem as faulty fuel pumps). Their response was, "well-then you will have to land at sea!" We just kept coming, and I suspect several of the crew said a little prayer. As we were about ten minutes out and dawn was just breaking, we got a call from the tower. "The fog has dissipated, you are cleared to land!" No landing ever felt so good-we were back home safely. We tied up to the boey, got pulled up to the ramp, and headed for the Ready room. As I laid on a table to get a little rest, news came on the radio. "President Roosevelt had just died!"

They replaced our fuel pumps and five days later we again took off for Kaneohe. This time all went well, it was a good flight. The Skipper decided I should Navigate. About 2,200 miles of water with no radio aids, but about 17 hrs later the Islands were in sight. It was really my first chance to do long range "dead reckoning" navigation. I was happy.

We spent about a month in Hawaii, doing various training flights and getting the crew to work together. Some of the crew spent their time playing poker and they invited me to join them. I was not really interested as I knew they were much better players than I was. I finally broke down and said, "I've got $20.00, when it's gone I quit. I'd win a little but mostly lost. When the $20.00 was gone—right in the middle of a hand—I quit. Never did play again.

We flew eight to ten hours practicing patrol flights and also an assortment of other things. Gunnery practice shooting at Sleeves Towed by other aircraft, anti sub work which was bombing Sleds towed by ships, practiced mine laying, etc. We were getting ready for our real mission.

These were the orders for us to leave for the war zone

Fleet Air Wing Two

Faw2/P16-4/00
Serial 2617

Br
22 May 1945

From: Commander Fleet Air Wing Two.
To: Lieut. (jg) George Edward Saxon, (al), USNR. (240548).
Via: Commanding Officer, Patrol Bombing Squadron ONE HUNDRED

Subject: Orders—Change of Duty.

1. On or about 26 May 1945, you and the officers enlisted men in your crew will regard yourselves detached from duty in Patrol Bombing Squadron ONE HUNDRED and from such other duties as may have been assigned. You will proceed, via aircraft assigned, to the port where Patrol Bombing Squadron THIRTEEN may be, and upon arrival deliver the aircraft and report to the Commanding Officer, Patrol Bombing Squadron THIRTEEN for duty involving flying in that Squadron.

2. The officers and enlisted men in your crew are:

   Lieut. (jg) Charles McCellian Dill, USN. (329437).

   Ensign Edward "N" Cooper, (al), USNR. (419751).

   Dougerty, Robert Owen, 617 71 37, AMM3c, V6, USNR.

   Hill, Harley Roy, 617 33 56, AOM2c V6 USNR.

   Johns, Charley Deley, 605 40 85, AOM3c, V6 USNR.

   KALL, Leonard Daniel, 859 91 18 ARM3c (T), V6, USNR.

   Kelly, James Dennis, 828 76 41, AMM3c (T), V6 USNR.

   Langharst, Lester (n), 251 03 67, SLc, V6, USNR.

   Mansfield, Charles Jr., 381 41 86, AMM2c, USN.

   Olshefski, Joseph John, 244 43 16, ARM3c, V6, USNR.

   Terrell, Donald Ivan, 321 63 11, ARM3c, USN.

3   The orders to duty in a part of the aeronautic organization of the Navy and the existing detail to duty involving flying remain in effect for you and the above listed officers.

4   Upon your reporting, the commanding officer, Patrol Bombing Squadron THIRTEEN (VPB-13) is hereby authorized to detach and order via first available Government air transportation to commander Fleet Air Wing Two, the crew relieved by you.

5   Copy to:

>   CNO (air)
>   BuPers
>   CinCPac   F. E. Bardwell,
>   ComServPac   Chief of Staff.
>   ComAirPac
>   ComFairWestCoast
>   ComAirPacSubComFwd
>   CFAW-1

On the 26th day of May we left Kaneohe for our final destination of Okinawa. We would "Island Hop" across the Pacific, stopping for fuel and rest. Our first leg was to Johnston Island, about a six hr. flight.

Johnston is nothing more than a Coral Reef sticking out of the ocean. It is large enough for a few buildings and a runway for land planes. The Harbor has Taxi ways and a runway dredged out of the Coral for Seaplanes. We had a good flight and were glad to be on our way. We tied up to a buoy and part of the crew went ashore for the night. When tied out to a buoy it was always mandatory for one Pilot and three crew to remain aboard the plane. The next morning the crew from ashore came aboard the plane and we prepared for take-off.

The Skipper was flying and I don't know if he had his eyes open or not. The runway was lined with buoys and you were supposed to take off between them, well he apparently got up on the wrong side of the buoys. He advanced the throttle and the plane started to move forward. Suddenly there was a tremendous "Crunch" in the Hull and the plane stopped. I ran down the ladder to the lower deck and there was Coral sticking up through the floorboards. We were high and dry with a large hole in our bottom. Thank goodness we stuck on the Coral or we would have sunk—we probably had a couple feet of water in the lower area.

Fortunately the Navy had a Barge with a large crane on it. They came out and hooked on to our sad looking PB2Y. As they lifted us off the Coral we stuffed mattresses into the hole. The crane could not lift our total weight so we had to pump water out as they moved us to the ramp. They pulled us out to a repair area and a maint. Crew went to work to put a temporary patch over the hole. We were surprised they had the material to put on as good a temporary patch fix as they did. We took quite a kidding from other crews who were stopping for fuel on their way west.

After two days of repair, we took off on the 29th headed for Kawajalein. This was a non-eventful ten hr. flight—we are now getting into the Pacific Islands that we had to win back from the Japs. Really, the only thing I remember about this stop-over was a visit to the Officer's Club. On the wall above the back-bar was a large picture of a beautiful nude lady. As the story went, a Pilot coming through had this picture of his wife and he lost it there. Sure bet he'd be shocked if he ever stopped there again

We laid over an extra night and on the thirty first took off for Saipan. This was another ten hr. flight and all went well. Saipan is a much larger Island and had much more facilities of all types. The loss of life was terrible in securing this area. It had become a major staging area for the western Pacific and the Air Force flew many flights to the mainland of Japan.

We were there almost two weeks while the repair crew put a new bottom on the Hull of our plane, I'd guess you would say we were "grounded". We were anxious to get going as we were to replace a crew that was going home. Finally on June 12th we received our final orders to report to V.P.B. 13, based on the Seaplane Tender "Kenneth Whiting". The ship was anchored (with many other ships) in a Harbor in a couple of Islands west of Okinawa. The area was called "Keramo Retto". It was a good nine hour flight on the 13th but we had to be much more alert as we were in the War Zone. These Islands had been secured but there was very intense fighting going on at Okinawa.

We found our ship, landed, and tied up to a buoy near it. We were the only PB2Y squadron there, but there were a couple of PBM (twin engine Seaplane) squadrons nearby. A boat came out to us, we loaded our gear aboard, and headed for our new home. I joined the Navy 2 ½ yrs. ago and I was finally aboard ship. Since we were over two weeks late, a couple of the crews didn't give us a very warm reception. We were now back together with crews and planes that we had trained with in San Diego.

The accommodations aboard the ship were not bad. We pilots bunked 2 to a room and we had good beds, not a lot of room to spare but it sure did beat living in a "Fox Hole"! Except for the "powdered eggs", the food was good. Only part of our time was spent aboard ship as there always had to be a pilot and three crew members aboard the plane when we were at anchor. The daytime watch wasn't as critical as the night watch. From sun down to sun up there was always someone on top of the plane with a sub-machine gun. This was because the Japs would try to swim out and destroy the planes. It was hard sometimes to wake someone for their watch—so the favorite thing to do was give them a blast with a fire extinguisher. We had two days to get organized and then on the sixteenth we had our first nine hour patrol over to the China Coast. We were looking for enemy shipping and submarines, also checking weather. Most of these patrols were "pie shaped" and other planes would fly other patrols—that way the whole area was covered.

Everyone has heard of all the suicide planes that Japan sent against U.S. ships. Well, we were right in the middle of that. Our second patrol was a twelve hour night flight—what we called "Picket Patrol". We flew north towards Japan and flew back and forth, spotting Japanese planes on our radar. We would radio back to home base, alerting them that these planes were on the way. We flew very low to the water, hoping the Japs would not see us. Most of the Jap planes flew with no lights, so did we. Early that morning, we heard a lot of chatter on the radio but could not figure out what was going on. As we got back home just after dawn, we saw smoke coming from the seaplane tender anchored next to us. We figured it must have been hit by a suicide plane. We tied up and our taxi boat picked us up—then we heard the news. Two planes had come in low over the Islands, one headed for that ship and one headed for ours. The other ship got hit, the bomb exploded where many were eating breakfast. There was much loss of life, I believe 50 or 60, but the fire was put out and the ship repaired. The other plane came towards our ship—many ships nearby were firing their guns at it. Just before the plane hit our ship, it was blown up. The engine apparently continued forward and put a large dent in the left side of our ship. Had it penetrated the side, aviation fuel and bombs inside would have blown the "Kenneth Whiting" sky high. As we got aboard ship we could see the damage everywhere—Bullets holes from all the guns firing at that plane. As we went up on deck there were pieces of the plane and pilot everywhere. I saw pieces of his shaved scalp and part of the scarf that they all wore. I picked up a couple pieces of plexi-glas canopy of the plane, that was enough. I could feel the shivers up and down my spine with the smell and thinking how bad it was, but it could have been so much worse. (The pieces of Plexi-glas are on display somewhere at the Naval Air Museum in Pensacola, Fla.) I don't believe anyone was killed on our ship—we sure came close to losing many good friends.

Our next couple patrols were up along the East Coast of Japan, about 40 or 50 miles out. We got within 300 miles of Tokyo. These were long flights, the ones where you sweat fuel on the way home. Many times we were out there to gather information that was used by others. We flew very low, not looking for enemy fighters. We did have depth charges aboard in the event we spotted a Jap sub. Knowing whose sub we spotted was sometimes a problem. We supposedly had info on where our subs were operating, but it was not always accurate. Also, they sometimes would not answer our call if they were on a mission that required radio silence. A couple flights later we did make a run on one of our own and fortunately they started screaming at us before we dropped a depth charge. We had a large Radome on top of the plane & some sophisticated Radar for those days. You might say we were the start of the A.W.A.C. planes.

I would like to mention our methods of Navigation. Many of our flights were 12 to 15 hours or longer, we never saw anything but ocean and we flew alone. There were no radio aids, nothing to "Home-in" on.

At night if the skies were clear, it was a "piece of cake". We would use a sextant and shoot a line on three different stars, or the moon. These would be plotted on a Navigation chart and where the lines crossed—that's where you are. You might shoot a "fix" every 15 or 20 minutes or once an hour, depending on conditions. These X's on the chart would give you the course and speed that you were flying. Remember, we normally flew at less than 1,000 ft. and you couldn't see the stars or moon if there was an overcast.

When this occurred, you navigated by dead reckoning. At night you would throw a flare out the rear hatch to check the drift. Drift is the effect the wind has on the heading of the plane.

Also, if you were flying at a few hundred feet, you might turn on the landing lights and try to observe the white caps on the water. With practice these two things would give you a pretty good estimate of the wind. As you can imagine, navigating at night in stormy weather sometimes called for an "extra Prayer"!

In the daytime you could shoot the sun for one line, but you also had to throw out smoke bombs to check the drift. Once again, reading the white caps was of tremendous value.

I have the deepest respect for our "Carrier Pilots" who navigated fully by dead recogning. After fighting a battle all over the sky, they had to come back and find a "postage stamp" to land on. That is why I was blessed to have gotten multi-engine duty.

Sometime along here one of our patrols was cut short due to an electrical fire in the Bow. We got it out by turning the power off, but a lot of wiring got scorched.

By the middle of July the fighting on Okinawa had pretty much died down. They moved us over to Buckner Bay on the East side of the Island. This gave us more protection from the weather, but we also had to be more vigilant of Japs swimming out to the planes. As luck would have it, two days later we were ordered to evacuate from a typhoon. About 80 seaplanes flew to Siapan to wait out the storm. We got back and flew a couple patrols to the China Coast and south to Formosa. We came across a small Merchant ship which we bombed and strafed.

Fortunately for us their gunners did not aim well. This was a late patrol and it was dark when we got back to Base. We probably were fifteen or twenty miles out when two of our Black Widow night fighters made a pass at us. Man, did they come close. We got on the radio to find out what was going on, just then they made another pass. This time they saw who we were, we did not know that our I.F.F. was not working. That is a radio signal sent out to identify yourself. We almost got shot down.

The next day we received orders to evacuate to Siapan. That typhoon had surprised everyone and turned and came back at us. The Bay had become extremely rough by the time we were ready to go. We should have had J.A.T.O. bottles to help us take off, but we didn't. We would get thrown into the air by one giant wave, only to fall back onto the next one. What kept the airplane from breaking apart, I'll never know. Finally one huge wave threw us into the air and we just hung on our props. Only by the "Grace of God" did we continue to fly and get out of there. It was a pretty stormy ride, the typhoon affected us most of the way.

About this time the Atomic bombs were dropped on Japan. We heard very little about it—we continued to fly mostly Picket Patrol South of Japan. The Japs were still sending many suicide planes South to get our ships. On one night flight we came across several of our Air Force planes that had become lost, and we directed them back to their base on Okinawa.

On the 14th of August while on patrol in the yellow Sea, we came across one of our subs who told us they had heard the war was over. When we got back to the ship we heard more news but it was very vague—no one seemed to really know what was going on. I remember that very night as I stood watch on top of our plane, a bright search light started to comb the sky. Finally, there it was, a Jap plane flying right above us—very high. No guns were fired and it turned and headed back home.

Being the Jr. pilot, I did not get to fly as much as the other two. That was o.k., as it really wasn't much fun to sit up there and turn knobs on the auto-pilot to keep us on course. Flying a plane as large as the "Coronado" really isn't much fun. Compare it to driving a "semi" instead of a sports car. Sure, I liked to fly—but I also enjoyed navigating.

We continued to fly patrols, mostly to the South Coast of Japan. Activity had really slowed down but we had to keep alert as there were some Japs that didn't want to quit fighting. On one flight to Southern Kyushu we counted forty six Jap planes just sitting on an airfield.

Squadron Skipper, John Ferguson, decided it was safe enough for us to go ashore on Okinawa and have a few "refreshments". It was quite an honor to set foot on soil that so many of our heroic men fought and died for. We didn't venture far from the beach, but one of their tombs was nearby. Okinawa was honeycombed with many caves, some were sealed off except for a small door. Inside were many urns filled with human bones—this was quite an experience. Glad I had a couple beers before I went in. This raised the hackles on a person's neck! It was a place worth trying not to remember for many days to come.

On Sept. fifteenth we flew a patrol to the China Coast and Shanghai. It is most vivid in my mind as we decided it was time to have some fun. We buzzed down the main streets of Shanghai at two hundred feet—people were running everywhere. We didn't tell many people about it. When we got back in that evening the weather looked bad and the sea was quite rough. I believe the weather man was sleeping. By morning the Bay was very rough with fifty mph. winds. A couple planes had already broken loose and washed up on the rocky beach. The orders finally came to evacuate to Cavite in the Philippines. It was a terrible take-off, once again the "Lord" lifted us out of that terrible sea. We saw some planes that appeared not to make it. We flew down to Cavite, a several hour flight and landed. Only then were we told that we were too late, there was no room for us. We were advised to fly down to the Naval Base at Jinimoc, Leyte. The weather had closed in, we knew this would be a rough trip. We could not fly over the mountains—the only route was through a narrow pass and we would be on instruments. The Skipper said to me, "Dill and I will fly the plane and you shall man the Radar!" Shortly after take-off we were in the "soup". It was up to me to tell them which way to turn. I was sweating a bit as the pass was narrow with several turns. After about twenty minutes we reached the other side of the mountains—the sky was beautiful and clear. Once again I was thankful for help from "Above" It was only a three hr. flight but those twenty minutes gave us all a couple gray hairs. It was quite a primitive spot, only a few buoys to tie up to. We got acquainted with some of the natives, couldn't speak their language but they showed us around. Naturally they had no refrigeration—the market just had raw meat hanging, mostly covered with flies. Fortunately we had food aboard the plane and were able to cook. Needless to say, we lived aboard the plane for our three day stay.

Speaking of food, we normally had ample food aboard for a few days, of course we received provisions from our ship—but we also would sometimes barter for canned meat, etc. from the Navy Sea-bees. We normally had access to liquor and they were very willing to trade. We had a galley so we could eat on our long flights.

Fortunately, when we were ready to leave the weather had cleared. How nice it was to fly through that pass and see what we came close to on our way down. And would you believe, that the radar that was our eyes in the bad weather—went out on our way back to Okinawa. When we arrived back we found out that twenty seven flying boats were lost in that storm—three were from our squadron, the rest were from the PBM squadron. Some crashed on take off, some sank at the buoys, and others washed up on the rocks. Then two days later, on Sept. twenty first—our ship and squadron moved to the Harbor at Sesabo, Japan. It was an instrument flight most of the way and we still had no Radar. We flew a couple flights around the southern part of Japan and found it really bombed to nothing, also hauled 2,500 pounds of mail from Sasebo to Nagasaki.

Just a week after moving, we were on the move again. We flew back to Okinawa to meet up with our ship—then took off that night for Cavite. We stayed there until the middle of Oct. while the Kenneth Whiting moved to Hong Kong, China.

Cavite was a friendly town across the bay from Manila. It had good seaplane facilities and we got quite a lot of "shore time".

We used to hang out at a bar called "The Bloody Bucket". They had live music and some pretty girls to dance with. When you walked down the street, it wasn't unusual to see two girls sitting on a porch picking lice out of each other's hair. We were fortunate to not have got them.

We were back in our own bunks aboard ship on the fourteenth. We started flying patrols out of Hong Kong—about a six hour flight—I really don't know why. Most were along the South East Coasts of China and French Indo China. We were anchored in Hong Kong Harbor—it was quite interesting. Of course it was a British Territory and they were not too fond of us. They didn't like us dancing with their Chinese girls. There were dance halls called "Taxi Dances". You could buy a strip of tickets and then give a girl a ticket to dance with her. If you got into a Rickshaw with a Chinese girl, the British guys would come after you and the guy pulling the Rickshaw had to run like crazy. At times it got pretty wild. The city was bombed out quite badly and much still laid in ruin. We were quite free to go ashore if we weren't flying. I even had to pull shore patrol duty a few times. We got acquainted with some girls who lived across the Bay in Kowloon. They invited us over and cooked us real Chinese food—no chop suey or chow mein. Many poor Chinese people live their whole lives on Sanpans—small flat boats. They would come to the stern of our ship and ask for food. We would throw coins into the water and they would dive for them. Life in the city seemed to have little value—I saw people laying dead on the sidewalk and no one gave them a second look. Also, sometimes you had to get off the sidewalk onto the street as that is where people dried their fish.

Between Patrol flights we would carry passengers and mail between Hong Kong and Cavite. One flight was eighteen passengers and mail—another was five passengers and 6,000 pounds of mail. On Nov. fourteenth I had a memorable flight, somebody else did the navigating and I flew the whole thing. We had five British Red Cross girls aboard on the way back to

Hong Kong and they took turns sitting in the right seat. Wow! "I was as happy as a Rooster with several hens". We flew a few more flights to Hinan and South Indo China—then the orders came through to get ready to head for home. That meant we had to have one last party at the little club we had set up in Hong Kong. We knew there was a lot of bad booze around, but one of the guys said he knew where to getgood stuff. We had one heck of a party, much was consumed. Before morning arrived, most everybody was sick. The bathrooms were a mess and the bunks were full. We were supposed to be getting ready to leave, the ship was ready to go, and all the pilots were sick. We were two days late leaving and the squadron Skipper really caught "Hell". That was about my twenty second birthday.

The last day of November we were well enough to fly and we took off for Cavite. That is the last we would see of the "Kenneth Whiting". Five and a half hours later the first leg of our flight was over and so was my time flying the PB2Y. The Skipper told me that it's a long way home and he trusted my navigating. The next morning the gas boat came out to refuel us and rammed the plane. Thank goodness it was just a dent and not a hole. Then we took off for a ten hour flight to Siapan. There were to be no lay over days, we wanted to go home.

We picked up several passengers in Siapan, they were PB2Y pilots from another squadron. Their planes had been towed out to sea and sunk and they wanted a ride home. We never found out why we were picked out to fly our planes back to the States. The next day we were on our way to the Island of Majuro, a twelve hour flight. This was a night landing among the coral reefs, a bit tricky since no one had been there before.

Fueled up early in the morning and we were airborne for Johnson Island. Remember that place, hopefully we won't have coral sticking through the bottom this time. Ten and a half hours and we were tied up to the boey and waiting for gas. It was now Dec. first—we had crossed the International Date Line and lost the day we had gained on the way out. The next day we left Johnson and six hours later set it down on the waters of Kaneohe Bay—we were back in the States again.

We spent about a week relaxing and doing some sightseeing. Went down to Wakiki Beach where the Royal Hawaiian and Moana hotels were the only two buildings—the rest was all sand. On the eleventh we took a short test hop, checking things out for the Trans-Pacific. On Dec. Fifteenth we took off for San Diego. We were told there was a storm front about half way but it should be no trouble. Once more, how wrong could the weather man be. Of course it was night and we could see it extended from the water to much higher then we could go. The Skipper got on the inter-com and said, "Coop, get on that Radar and find us a hole"! We flew North and South along that front for almost an hour—using up precious fuel and getting no closer to home. I truly believe a few Prayers were being said. All of a sudden I thought I saw a thin spot and I told Saxon and Dill, head into it. It was a rough ride but we made it through. Now all I had to do was figure where we were. I gave them a heading and we were on our way. Mansfield, The plane Capt. told me how much fuel he figured we had left and I plotted that against the estimated flight time—it would be close. The weather was good and we had a little tail wind, and that helped. Also this time the Harbor was reported clear, no fog. What a relief when the Coast line showed up on Radar, we would make it. What a sweet landing, the best one ever. We had been in the air well over seventeen hours and we still had a little fuel left. I quickly added up the miles since we left Hong Kong—7872 miles. No doubt I will never navigate again, will I ever fly? I ended with 1,053 logged hours. We were proud to have brought our plane back safely.

When we checked in at North Island they told us that we would be mustered out right there. Well, I had a girl friend in Oklahoma that I had met when I was in Navigation Training and I kinda wanted to see her. I called my folks and told them to send my dress uniforms to her address—I'd stop there and then come on home.

We spent several days going through paper work & getting us all checked out with the gear we had been issued. We just hung around waiting for them to decide what they were going to do. Finally we got word that they had changed their minds and that we were going to be mustered out at Great Lakes, Ill. Oh boy, that's the Navy for you. I had to call my folks and tell them of the change then call Oklahoma for her to send my uniforms back home. They gave us train tickets and sent us on our way. I don't know how long it took but it wasn't a bad ride—much nicer than when we rode cattle cars. Of course at Great Lakes it took a couple days to get through the paper work. I called my folks and they came and picked me up—got a—Ford-Tri Motor ride back to the Island with my old friend Milton Hershberger. I believe I got home a couple days before Christmas. My active duty was actually terminated in early Feb. 1946, when I was promoted to Lt. J.G. I signed up to stay in the reserves and did some training at

Gross ele, Michigan N.A.S. and continued to take correspondence Courses, etc. for many years. I was finally Honorably Discharged from the U.S. Navy on June 19th, 1962—about 4 months short of twenty years.

Note—I found out years later that all of the PB2Y Coronados that our Squadron flew back, were towed out off Point Loma and sunk. What a shame—I do hope the fish are enjoying the scenery. The only PB2Y in existence is at the Naval Air Museum at Pensacola, Fla. This is a transport model, purchased by Howard Hughs to train pilots to fly the "Spruce Goose". After he died, it was found in a barn near L.A. Harbor. It was barged to Pensacola. We pray that it will get restored and not torn up by a hurricane.

A Little History

In the 1930's four engine flying boats were used to fly the newly established air routes across the Pacific. The Navy was using a two engine flying boat, the PBY "Catatina"—mainly for patrol and rescue.

The "High Brass" decided that a larger flying boat was needed, one with longer range and greater load capacity.

Both Sikorsky, who had much experience in building flying boats, and Consolidated Aircraft Company, who built the PBY, decided to build an experimental model to the Navy's specifications. Sikorsky's VS-44A "Excaliber" was found to have some undesirable stall characteristics and the contract was awarded to Consolidated with their XPB2Y-1 "Coronado".

In 1938 the first XPB2Y-1 was launched and flight testing started with Consolidated and Navy and after more testing, was accepted. Now Pilots and crews must be trained to fly and maintain these large flying boats.

In mid 1940, "VP13" was officially commissioned, and became an active training and patrol Squadron. In 1941 the PB2Y-2 joined the squadron. This version had many added features and was described as a real "work horse"! Several crews were trained, but on Dec. 7 1941 the squadron only had three planes. That night all planes were readied and the next morning two PB2Y2's took off on patrol off the west coast. The "Big Boats" had entered war service. Also one plane was ordered ready to fly to Pearl Harbor, Hawaii—A top secret flight with Secretary of the Navy, Frank Knox, aboard.

Production was stepped up and more planes joined the squadron. Since there were not many land planes flying the long ocean flights and few landing fields were available, the Big Boats were in demand. For many of the "High Brass," this was their favorite method of transportation. Also, flying vital information or parts became routine. Of course there always were patrols to fly to check on Jap activity and weather. Most planes were equipped with nose, top, and tail turrets with twin 50 Cal. Guns. Also a single 50 cal. Waist gun on each side, Bombs, depth charge, and torpedo racks were available when needed. A few planes were converted to carry passengers or stretchers for medical evac.

As time went by, some crews were called on to drop bombs on Jap held Islands or shipping. This was a very scary mission but had quite good results with little loss of equip. or crews. As the war progressed across the Pacific, so did VP 13. Soon the designation was changed to VPB 13. Seaplane tenders became the crews home. At first they were ships converted to serve the purpose—later ships were built especially for this use.

The larger tenders had a flat deck near the stern & a huge crane for lifting the planes aboard if they could not be serviced on the water. As well as living quarters, the ship provided our supplies, ammo, bombs, fuel, etc.

When I joined the VPB at North Island N.A.S. in Jan. 1945, we were flying the PB2Y-5. It had much improved Radar and other modifications from the earlier models. Our mission, based in the Okinawa area, was mostly patrol—much of it along the South Coast of Japan on Anti—Kamikaze flights. We would spot them on Radar and notify the fleet what was coming. We did have some contact with enemy shipping, but most of that was now being done by the Navy's PB4Y's—the Navy's version of the B24. Airstrips on some of the Islands we had captured now allowed them to operate.

After the war we flew passengers, mail, and of course continued weather patrols. Our last Base of Operations was Hong Kong, China. We arrived Oct. 14th 1945 and departed for home Nov. 29th. Some lay overs along the way, but arrived N.A.S. North Island on Dec.15 1945.

Corondo PB2Y dimentions:
    Wing span—115'
    Length—85'
    Height—27' 6"
    4—Pratt & Whitney R 1830 engines
    Empty weight—approx. 41,000 lbs.
    Max. weight—approx. 68,000 lbs.
    Range—approx.—2500 mi. with aux. tanks.
    Speed—approx.—175 MPH, depending on weight.

After the war I sort of lost interest in flying. I probably could have gotten unlimited multi engine land and sea, plus instrument, rating but I chose to go into business with my family in the wine and restaurant business. (I had done my thing). We were very busy planting more vineyards and erecting a new building.

A couple years later we had a very cold winter and there was very good ice fishing around the Islands. Renting fishing shantys was a big business for the Island men. Of course, all the fishermen had to be flown over from the Mainland in the Ford Tri-Motors of Island Airlines.

Milt Hershberger, my old boss from years before, called me and asked if I wanted to come to work during this busy time. Since it was too cold to prune grapes and there was not much cellar work to do, (The restaurant was closed during winter) I accepted. Here I was back at my old pre-war job, hauling mail, selling tickets, loading passengers, and whatever. I didn't relish getting up at 4 a.m. and going out into that zero weather. We started to fly at 6 a.m., but first we had to start the engine heaters and get that iron warm so the oil would flow. The hangers were not heated, only one had doors. One morning I mentioned to Milt that it sure was cold. His reply, "Oh, it just puts pep in your step". This was great business for the Airline.

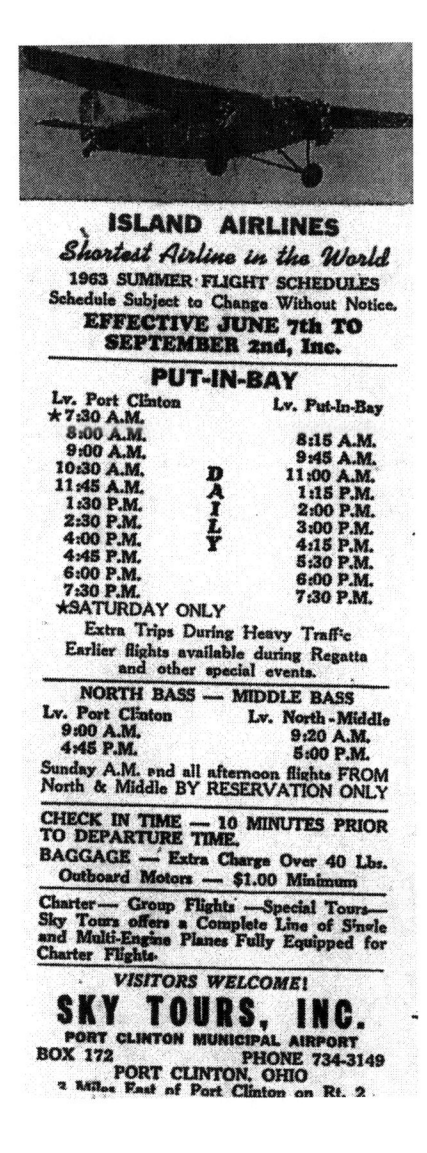

ISLAND AIRLINES
Shortest Airline in the World
1963 SUMMER FLIGHT SCHEDULES
Schedule Subject to Change Without Notice.
EFFECTIVE JUNE 7th TO SEPTEMBER 2nd, Inc.

PUT-IN-BAY

Lv. Port Clinton		Lv. Put-In-Bay
★7:30 A.M.		
8:00 A.M.		8:15 A.M.
9:00 A.M.		9:45 A.M.
10:30 A.M.	D	11:00 A.M.
11:45 A.M.	A	1:15 P.M.
1:30 P.M.	I	2:00 P.M.
2:30 P.M.	L	3:00 P.M.
4:00 P.M.	Y	4:15 P.M.
4:45 P.M.		5:30 P.M.
6:00 P.M.		6:00 P.M.
7:30 P.M.		7:30 P.M.

★SATURDAY ONLY

Extra Trips During Heavy Traffic
Earlier flights available during Regatta and other special events.

NORTH BASS — MIDDLE BASS

Lv. Port Clinton	Lv. North - Middle
9:00 A.M.	9:20 A.M.
4:45 P.M.	5:00 P.M.

Sunday A.M. and all afternoon flights FROM North & Middle BY RESERVATION ONLY

CHECK IN TIME — 10 MINUTES PRIOR TO DEPARTURE TIME.
BAGGAGE — Extra Charge Over 40 Lbs.
Outboard Motors — $1.00 Minimum

Charter — Group Flights — Special Tours — Sky Tours offers a Complete Line of Single and Multi-Engine Planes Fully Equipped for Charter Flights.

VISITORS WELCOME!
SKY TOURS, INC.
PORT CLINTON MUNICIPAL AIRPORT
BOX 172   PHONE 734-3149
PORT CLINTON, OHIO
2 Miles East of Port Clinton on Rt. 2

Ticket sales were rather unique. I had a board with 6 pins sticking up. On each pin were 15—4 inch square metal plates. Each stack was a different color, Each color was a plane load. On a good weekend morning we might fly as many as 200 fishermen to the Islands. That's a few trips for 2 Ford Tri-Motors. It went like clock work, usually, with the rush pretty well over by the time for the first scheduled flight at 8:30. The flight took about 9 minutes each way, the props.

Never stopped turning. For most it was one day of fishing, but some would stay over. Sunday afternoon was really a "rat race", trying to get them all back before dark. I might add that the isles of the Ford Tri-Motor would get very slippery, covered with frozen fish slime. Fish were not put on a stringer or put in a cooler, they were put into a 100 pound burlap feed sack. Yes, sometimes those sacks would be pretty full when fishing was good. That was part of my job, melting it out and getting cleaned up for the next morning.

I did a lot of airplane riding and would get some right seat stick time when we had no passengers aboard. The urge of flying was starting to come back. Harold Hauck, Milt's other pilot, who had 14,000 hours in the Ford (That's about 70,000 take offs and landings), wanted me to get my commercial license and help them out in the winter. It sounded good, so I passed my written exam and my physical and was building up some flight time. The plane I was using got rented out to a couple guys who decided to land on the ice near some fish shanty. They hit an ice cake and washed out the landing gear. Ice fishing ended before it was repaired and I had to go back to the family business. The idea sort of cooled and I decided if I didn't fly all the time, I had no business flying.

I just got my Private License and did fly once in a while. One day I decided to take my three year old son and his mom for a ride. We took off and headed across the lake for the Mainland. This was tandem trainer and it had dual controls. About half way across, the engine suddenly went to idle. As I was starting to check things, my wife said, "Greg pulled something back here". I guess he wanted to help, he had pulled the throttle lever back. Needless to say, I kept my hand on my throttle control the rest of the flight. I quit flying soon after that—it was the mid 50s.

I have never lost my love for airplanes, especially the old propeller jobs with round engines. Just after we were married I told Vivian, "If airplanes could cook, wash, and do all the nice things a woman does, I might have married an airplane"! She didn't think that was too funny. By the time this goes to print I should have had one of my last wishes—a ride in a "Stearman," that's an open cockpit Bi-plane that I flew in training, and similar to the Waco that I had my first ride in when I was 7 yrs. old. That is what started it all.

A little extra:
From the Lakes to the Pacific
Was the life that I dreamed of
To fly in the clouds was terrific
A Waco was the plane for above

I was just a small true Island boy
With a hero that flew a red Waco
I realized that plane was not a toy
I knew him and felt I was macho

I graduated from the High School
I had the picture of the plane I'd get
My parents taught the Golden Rule
And no money to give for this pet

When the war broke out in the 40's
I knew I would fly for Uncle Sam
Nothing to do with being sporty
I didn't think about flying to Japan

I exited the training with flying colors
I marched with pride to get my wings
head high, I paid no heed to others
The Brass pinned as the crowd sings

I wrote to fly a Multi engine plane
My delight they granted my desire
The PB2Y controls we had to train
A hot shot pilot was the head flyer

I wore my white Officer's uniform
They sent me to navigation school
I studied hard and waved the storm
I loved flying, but navigation is cool

We flew that four engine plane to China
We flew above the waters a thousand feet
At times the waters were rough, kinda
Especially when landing on a coral reef

I love flying the stearman so much more
Even now at age eighty five I run to see
That beautiful plane that I always adore
The open cockpit double wings so free

I will take a ride in one soon
I don't care what color it is
Wind in my face back at noon
To enjoy every moment of bliss.

By Rev. Vivian Cooper

End of Book